TO:

FROM:

simple truths®
Motivational & Inspirational Gifts

Published by Simple Truths, LLC and SUCCESS Books
1952 McDowell Road, Suite 300
Naperville, Illinois 60563
800-900-3427
www.simpletruths.com
Simple Truths is a registered trademark.

SUCCESS | BOOKS
WWW.SUCCESS.COM

www.SUCCESS.com
SUCCESS is a registered trademark and SUCCESS Books is a trademark of R&L
Publishing, Ltd.

Published in association with Yates &Yates: www.yates2.com

Based on *Put Your Dream to the Test* by John C. Maxwell.

Published with permission from Thomas Nelson Publishers.

Printed and bound in the United States of America.

Book design by Brian Frantz

Edited by J.M. Emmert

04 WOZ 13

OWN *Your* DREAMS

Discovering Your Purpose in life

JOHN C. MAXWELL

Contents

It's never too late to be
what you might
have been.

George Eliot

Introduction

What is your **dream?**
How will you **achieve it?**

The first question **may be difficult to answer.** You may have many dreams. Yet, there must be one that stands out above all others...one that inspires you, energizes you, and empowers you to do everything you can to achieve it.

The second question **is the reason most people never realize their dreams.** They have no strategy in place for attaining it, no knowledge of what is needed and must be sometimes sacrificed to have the dream come true.

Will you achieve your dreams in your lifetime?

I'm certain that you desire to. I'm sure you hope you will. But will you actually do it? What odds would you give yourself? One in five? One in a hundred? One in a million? How can you tell whether your chances are good or whether your dream will always remain exactly that—a dream?

Most people have no idea how to achieve their dreams. What they possess is a vague notion that there is something they would like to do someday or someone they would like to become. But they don't know how to get from here to there. If that describes you, then you'll be glad to know that there really is hope.

Dreams come a size
too big so we can grow
into them.

—Josie Bisset

PART I:

What Is Your Dream?

Dreams are valuable commodities.

They propel us forward. They give us energy. They make us enthusiastic. Everyone ought to have a dream. But what if you're not sure whether you have a dream you want to pursue?

I've studied successful people for 40 years. I've known hundreds of high-profile people who achieved big dreams. And I've achieved a few dreams of my own. What I've discovered is that a lot of people have misconceptions about dreams.

A genuine dream is a picture and blueprint of a person's purpose and potential. Or as my friend Sharon Hull says, "A dream is the seed of possibility planted in the soul of a human being, which calls him to pursue a unique path to the realization of his purpose."

Sadly, far too many people have dreams that are not genuine, but simply wishful thinking that fills their thoughts but will never fulfill their lives. **Take a look at the following examples of "dreamers" who are unlikely to see their dreams come to fruition.**

Daydreamers

Their dreams are *merely distractions*
from their current work.

Pie-in-the-Sky Dreamers

Their dreams are *wild ideas*
with no strategy or basis in reality.

Bad Dreamers

Their dreams are worries that breed
fear and paralysis.

Idealistic Dreamers

Their dreams are images of the way
the world *would be*...
if they were in charge.

Vicarious Dreamers

Their dreams are lived
through others.

Romantic Dreamers

Their dreams are based on the belief
that *others* will make them happy.

Career Dreamers

Their dreams are based on the belief
that *career success*
will make them happy.

Destination Dreamers

Their dreams are based on the belief
that a ***position, title, or award***
will make them happy.

Material Dreamers

Their dreams are based on the belief
that *wealth or possessions*
will make them happy.

Seasonal Dreamers

They mistake *short-term targets*
for genuine dreams.

If you are one of these dreamers, I want you to know that there's good news.

You can reshape your dream.

You can overcome obstacles.

You can live your dream.

Five Common Roadblocks

The minute you settle for less than you deserve, you get even less than you settled for.

Maureen Dowd

If you've given up hope, lost sight of your dream, or never connected with something that you think is worth dreaming and working toward, perhaps it would help you to learn about the **five most common reasons why** people have trouble identifying their dreams.

Roadblock 1

Being Discouraged from Dreaming by Others

Many people have had their dreams knocked right out of them! **The world is filled with dream crushers and idea killers.** Some people who aren't pursuing any dreams of their own don't like to see others pursuing theirs. Others' success makes them feel inadequate or insecure.

Perhaps others have dragged you down in life. They've discouraged you from dreaming. Maybe they resented the fact that you wanted to move up or do something significant with your life. Or maybe they were trying to protect you from pain or disappointment. Either way, you've been discouraged from dreaming. Take heart. It's never too late to start dreaming and pursuing your dreams.

Roadblock 2

Being Hindered by Past Disappointments and Hurts

Disappointment is the gap that exists between expectation and reality. All of us have encountered that gap. We've had unexpectedly bad experiences. We've had to live with our unfulfilled desires and had our hopes dashed.

Disappointments can be highly damaging to us.

Novelist Mark Twain observed, **"We should be careful to get out of an experience only the wisdom that is in it**—and stop there; lest we be like the cat that sits down on a hot stove lid. She will never sit down on a hot stove lid again—and that is well; but also she will never sit down on a cold one anymore."

Roadblock 3

The Habit of Settling for Average

Dreams require a person to stretch, to go beyond average. **You can't reach for a dream and remain safely mediocre at the same time.** The two are incompatible.

When we are too uninspired to dream, when we settle for average, we may be tempted to blame it on others, on our circumstances, on the system.But the truth is that mediocrity is always a personal choice.

Roadblock 4

Lack of Confidence

Humor columnist Erma Bombeck observed, "It takes a lot of courage to show your dreams to someone else." It takes confidence to talk about a dream and even more to pursue it. And sometimes **confidence separates the people who dream and pursue those dreams from those who don't.**

Self-confidence is vital to success.

In a study of children, Karen Greno-Malsch found that lower self-worth translated into 37 percent less willingness to negotiate and use of 11 percent fewer negotiation strategies with others. She also discovered that the greater a child's self-worth, the greater the willingness to incur the risks of prolonged negotiation and the greater the adaptability. In other words, **the more confidence you have in yourself, the less likely you are to give up trying to get what you want.**

Roadblock 5

Lack of Imagination to Dream

How do people discover their dreams? By dreaming! That may sound overly simplistic, but that's where it starts. **Imagination is the soil that brings a dream to life.** Nobel Prize–winning physicist Albert Einstein, a dreamer and thinker, understood the value of the imagination. He said, "When I examine myself and my methods of thought, I come to the conclusion that the gift of fantasy has meant more to me than my talent for absorbing positive knowledge." Einstein called his imagination a "holy curiosity."

If you come from a discouraging background, or you don't think of yourself as an especially imaginative person, don't lose hope. You can still discover and develop a dream. God has put that ability in every one of us.

Always
remember there
are only two kinds of
people in this world—the
realists and the dreamers.
The realists know where they're
going. The dreamers have
already been there.

Robert Orben

Preparing Your Dream

If you are unsure of what your dream might be—either because you are afraid to dream or because you somehow lost your dream along the way—then **start preparing yourself to receive your dream by doing six things** to put yourself in the best possible position to receive a dream.

Once you do these six things, focus on discovering your dream. As you do, keep in mind the words of my agent Matt Yates, who says,

"A dream is what you desire if anything and everything is possible."

Mental Preparation:

Read and **study** in areas of
your greatest interest.

Experiential Preparation:

Engage in *activities* in areas related to your interests.

Visual Preparation:

Put up *pictures of people and things* that inspire you.

Hero Preparation:

Read about and try to *meet people you admire* and who inspire you.

Physical Preparation:

Get your ***body in optimal shape***
to pursue your dream.

Spiritual Preparation:

Seek *God's help* for
a bigger-than-self dream.

God will help you be
all you can be, but He
will never help you be
someone else.

Joyce Meyer

Owning Your Dream

Think about your personal history. **How have your plans, goals, and desires been influenced by others?** Are you aware of how your vision for yourself has been impacted? Is it possible that your dreams are the result of who your parents think you are? Who others think you are? Who you wish you were? Or are they the result of who you really are and are meant to be?

It is the responsibility of every individual to sort that out for himself or herself. In fact, you will fulfill your dream and live the life for which God created you only after you figure it out.

As Nobel Prize winner for literature Joseph Brodsky observed, **"One's task consists first of all in mastering a life that is one's own, not imposed or prescribed from without, no matter how noble its appearance may be.** For each of us is issued but one life, and we know full well how it all ends. It would be regrettable to squander this one chance on someone else's appearance, someone else's experience."

How do you know whether you're pursuing a dream that's not really your dream? Here are some clues to help you figure it out:

When Someone Else Owns Your Dream

It will not have the right fit.

It will be a weight on your shoulders.

It will drain your energy.

It will put you to sleep.

It will take you out of your strength zone.

It will be fulfilling to others.

It will require others to make you do it.

When You Own Your Dream

It will feel right on you.

It will provide wings to your spirit.

It will fire you up.

It will keep you up at night.

It will take you out of your comfort zone.

It will be fulfilling to you.

You will feel you were made to do it.

When the dream is right for the person and the person is right for the dream, they cannot be separated from each other. **If something is truly your dream, you need to see the possibility it represents—and you need to own it!** Philosopher Søren Kierkegaard asserted, "A possibility is a hint from God. One must follow it."

The most common excuse for not owning and pursuing a dream is timing. Some say it's too soon. **The timing will never be perfect for you to pursue your dream, so you might as well start now.** If you don't, then next year you'll be a year older and not a step closer to it. If you're willing to take that step—to start owning your dream—then begin the process by doing the following:

Be Willing to Bet on Yourself

You may succeed if nobody else believes in you, but **you will never succeed if you don't believe in yourself.** In fact, if you can't believe in yourself, you will have a difficult time believing in much of anything else. You will be adrift in the world with nothing compelling you to move forward. **People who take ownership of their dreams believe in themselves,** and when they believe in themselves, they are willing to bet on themselves.

Lead Your Life Instead of Just Accepting Your Life

The power of choice is the greatest power that a person possesses. Oprah Winfrey confirms this power and encourages people to make the most of it:

"Understand that the right to choose your own path is a sacred privilege. Use it. Dwell in possibility." Unfortunately many people just accept their lives—they don't become leaders of themselves. As a result, they can't get out of their own way.

Love What You Do
and Do What You Love

Successful people—those who see and seize their dream—love what they do and do what they love. They allow their passion and talent to guide them. Why? Because **talent, purpose, and potential always come hand in hand.** I don't believe that God makes mistakes. He doesn't create people to be talented in one area but interested in an unrelated one. There is always a potential alignment of talent and passion if we have the courage to pursue our purpose and take risks.

Don't Compare Yourself (or Your Dream) to Others

Success is doing the best you can with what you have wherever you start in life. **You should never let others set the standard for you, just as you should never try to live someone else's dream.**

Comparing ourselves to others doesn't benefit us, nor does it get us any closer to living our dream. When we play the comparison game, we're like the cows in the pasture that see a milk truck go by with a sign that says, "Pasteurized, homogenized, standardized, vitamin A added." One cow says to the other, "Makes you feel sort of inadequate, doesn't it?"

Believe in Your Vision for the Future Even When Others Don't Understand You

Though you have great potential and the seed of purpose in you, **others will not necessarily understand you**. **Don't let that dissuade you from taking ownership of your dream** and moving forward. If your dream is really your dream, then it will seem outrageous to more than a few people.

Only those who
see their dream
are able to seize
their dream.

John C. Maxwell

PART II:

How Will You Achieve It?

If you want to accomplish a dream, you will be able to do so only when you can see it clearly. You must define it before you can pursue it. **Most people don't do that.** Their dreams remain dreams—fuzzy and unspecific. As a result, they never achieve them.

Pursuing a dream that isn't clear would be like someone who loves cowboy movies launching out on a trip to the West and then driving in that direction, hoping to run into something interesting.

Instead, the person would need to turn that vague notion into specifics, saying something like, "I want to visit the National Cowboy and Western Heritage Museum in Oklahoma City; then travel to Arizona to see the O.K. Corral in Tombstone; visit Old Tucson to see where they filmed *Rio Bravo*, my favorite western; and see beautiful Monument Valley, where movies such as *Stagecoach* and *Once Upon a Time in the West* were filmed." Now that can be accomplished!

If you want to achieve your dream, you need to bring it into focus. As you do, here are some **things to keep in mind:**

A Clear Dream Makes a General Idea Very Specific

A dream that isn't clear won't help you get anywhere.

What do you want to accomplish? What do you want to experience? What do you want to contribute? Who do you want to become? In other words, **what does success look like for you? If you don't define it, you won't be able to get where you want to go.**

It sounds overly simple, but a primary reason why most people don't get what they want is that they don't *know* what they want. They haven't defined their dream in clear and compelling detail.

A Clear Dream Doesn't Become Clear without Effort

It doesn't take much effort to let your mind drift and dream. However, **it takes *great* effort to set your mind to the task of developing a clear and compelling dream.** Take the effort to bring clarity to your dream using your own tools and method.

A clear picture of a dream may come to you all at once, in lightning bolt fashion, but for most people it doesn't work that way. Most people need to keep working at it, clarifying it, redrawing it. If the process is difficult, that's no reason to give up. In fact, if it's too easy, maybe you're not dreaming big enough. Just keep working at it because a clear dream is worth fighting for.

A Clear Dream Affirms Your Purpose

Bringing your dream into focus should confirm the sense that you are going in the right direction, and it should strengthen your sense of purpose.

A person's dream and purpose are intertwined. God designs us to *want* to do what we are most capable of doing. Because of this, when we do things that are making an impact, something resonates within us.

A Clear Dream Determines Your Priorities

It's easy to get so caught up in the day-to-day process of life that you lose sight of the big picture. However, **when your dream is clearly in sight, it helps you get your priorities straight.**

Nobody can have it all. We like to think we can, but we can't. If you see your dream clearly—and keep it in front of you continually—it will help you understand what you must sacrifice and what you must dedicate yourself to in order to keep moving forward. **Only a clear picture of who you are and where you want to go can help you prioritize what you need to do.** We all make choices. Clarity of vision creates clarity of priorities.

A Clear Dream Gives Direction and Motivation to the Team

Your big dream will undoubtedly require the participation of other people. If you are part of an organization that has goals or vision, then you must work with other people in order to accomplish them. Either way, **you must be capable of working with a team.**

That can be done effectively only when you possess a clear picture of what you want to achieve.

Lack of clarity hinders initiative, inhibits persistence, and undermines follow-through. Followers don't give their best to something they don't understand. People don't stay on course for something they cannot see. Nobody becomes motivated by something he kinda, sorta believes in.

Shallow men believe in luck. ...Strong men believe in cause and effect.

John C. Maxwell

Building Your Dream

As you move forward in the pursuit of your dream, you need to ask yourself, **"Am I depending on factors within my control to achieve my dream?"** **People who build their dreams on reality take a very different approach to dreams than people who live in Fantasyland.** Take a look at how differently they approach achieving a dream.

Fantasizers . . .

Rely on luck.

Focus on the destination.

Cultivate unhealthy expectations.

Minimize the value of work.

Look for excuses.

Create inertia.

Breed isolation.

Wait.

Avoid personal risks.

Dream Builders . . .

Rely on discipline.

Focus on the journey.

Cultivate healthy discontent.

Maximize the work they do.

Lead to action.

Generate momentum.

Promote teamwork.

Initiate.

Embrace risk as necessary.

People who are successful in the long run don't leave everything to chance. They focus on what they can do, and then they do it. **To achieve your dream, you not only need to work hard for it, but you also have to make sure it plays to your strengths.** That means knowing what you can and cannot do.

The first step in facing reality requires you to look at yourself realistically, to **see yourself as you truly are.** The nature of self-evaluation has a profound effect on a person's values, beliefs, thinking processes, feelings, needs, and goals. **Focus on doing the things you love to do and building on your strengths.**

Building on Your Strengths Activates the Law of Least Effort

When you build on your strengths, the activities using those strengths come more easily to you.

When people are going with their strengths and working in their sweet spot, the work they do is simple and easy. However, when they're focusing their effort in an area of weakness, what they do is complex and difficult. **To achieve your dream, you have to build on strengths.**

Building on Your Strengths Enables Consistently Good Results

Dreams don't come true because a person does something well once in a while. **Success isn't an event— it's a lifestyle. Dreams are fulfilled when someone performs with excellence day after day.** That comes only if you work within an area of strength.

You cannot achieve success without consistency. You cannot achieve consistency if you are working outside your strengths. It will take all the talent you have to achieve a big dream. Following that talent will give you the greatest chance to be consistently good at what you do.

Building on Your Strengths Gives You the Highest Return

Successful people always put their time, energy, and resources into their strengths because they receive the highest return from it. And when they occasionally depart from that approach, the result is mediocrity.

You have some wonderful strengths that make you unique and hold great possibilities for your future. You just have to find them.

Saddle your dreams before you ride them.

Mary Webb

Securing Your Dream

To achieve your dream, you must plan. **A strategy is as important a part of the dream as the dream itself.** Most people would agree that planning is important. However, they still neglect to do it. They forget to make it part of the process. We're so busy stargazing that we neglect strategizing.

Here's an approach to planning that can assist you, based on the word *secure*.

SECURE

SECURE

State All Your Positions

The process of reaching your dream is like reaching a destination using a GPS device. If it knows where you are and you tell it where you want to go, it can create a map for you. The difference between a GPS and you is that you have to create all of your own turn-by-turn directions.

As you begin to write out the steps you think you must take to reach your dream, don't expect to be able to follow them quickly and easily. **Plans are clear and simple. Life and the pursuit of dreams are messy.**

SECURE

xamine All Your Actions

The real difference between a dream and wishful thinking is what you do day to day.

In the beginning, you just need to get moving. Try different things. **It's much easier to start doing something right if you've already started doing something.**

SECURE

Consider All Your Options

Once you figure out a plan for reaching your dream—the intermediate steps you think will get you there—there is a danger that you will become inflexible and try to stick to your plan no matter what. Sometimes it's wiser to explore other options. **When you are having a hard time moving forward, don't be quick to revise your dream. Instead revise your plan.**

British Prime Minister Winston Churchill, a gifted orator and an inspired leader, said about strategy: "However beautiful the strategy, you should occasionally look at the results." **The results matter. What good is a masterfully planned strategy that doesn't yield positive results?**

SEC**U**tilize All Your Resources

Think about your dream. Maybe you want to win an Olympic medal or build a great company or raise your children so that they reach their potential. No matter the dream, it will require resources. What's available to you? What assets do you possess? Who can help you? Stop and make a list. **It's not enough to just plan.**

You need to engage every resource you have in order to make your dream come true.

Remove All Your Nonessentials

You will have to give up things to achieve your dream. And the greatest challenge isn't giving up the obvious things that will hurt you. It will be giving up the good things that you like but that won't help you.

Removing nonessentials from your daily routine will be a constant struggle, but it is worth fighting for. Why? Because most people who fail to reach their dreams aren't stopped because insurmountable barriers confronted them. No, they often become worn out trying to carry too many things on their journeys.

SECURE

Embrace All Your Challenges

Once you've stated all your positions, examined all your actions, considered all your options, utilized all your resources, and removed all your nonessentials, you still have one more thing to do: **embrace all your challenges**. King Solomon, considered the wisest man who ever lived, wrote, **"A sensible man watches for problems ahead and prepares to meet them.** The simpleton never looks and suffers the consequences."

Choosing to lead
your life and not just
accepting it is critical to
owning your dream.

Holocaust survivor Elie Wiesel wrote in *Souls on Fire* that when you die and you go to meet your Maker, you're not going to be asked why you didn't become a messiah or find a cure for cancer. All you're going to be asked is, "Why didn't you become you? Why didn't you become all that you are?"

Reaching your God-given potential requires taking responsibility for yourself and your life. **It means taking an active leadership role with yourself.**

How do you do that? By saying yes—to yourself, to hope, to your dream. **Every time you say yes, you open yourself up to your potential and to greater possibilities.** If you're used to saying "no," you may find it difficult. If that is true in your case, then at least be willing to say "maybe" to yourself. **Never forget that you are a miracle, that you are unique, possessing talents, experiences, and opportunities that no one else has ever had—or will ever have.** It is your responsibility to become everything that you are, not only for your benefit but also for everyone else's.

Your dream.
See it.
Seize it.
Keep it alive.

Dream Summary

5 Common Roadblocks

ROADBLOCK 1:

Being Discouraged from Dreaming by Others

ROADBLOCK 2:

Being Hindered by Past Disappointments and Hurts

ROADBLOCK 3:

The Habit of Settling for Average

ROADBLOCK 4:

Lack of Confidence

ROADBLOCK 5:

Lack of Imagination to Dream

6 Ways to Prepare for Your Dream

1. MENTAL PREPARATION.
Read and study in areas of your greatest interest.

2. EXPERIENTIAL PREPARATION.
Engage in activities in areas related to your interests.

3. VISUAL PREPARATION.
Put up pictures of people and things that inspire you.

4. HERO PREPARATION.
Read about and try to meet people you admire and who inspire you.

5. PHYSICAL PREPARATION.
Get your body in optimal shape to pursue your dream.

6. SPIRITUAL PREPARATION.
Seek God's help for a bigger-than-self dream.

5 WAYS TO START OWNING YOUR DREAM

1. Be Willing to Bet on Yourself

2. Lead Your Life Instead of Just Accepting Your Life

3. Love What You Do and Do What You Love

4. Don't Compare Yourself (or Your Dream) to Others

5. Believe in Your Vision for the Future Even When Others Don't Understand You

5 Reasons to Keep Your Dream in Focus

1. A Clear Dream Makes a General Idea Very Specific

2. A Clear Dream Doesn't Become Clear without Effort

3. A Clear Dream Affirms Your Purpose

4. A Clear Dream Determines Your Priorities

5. A Clear Dream Gives Direction and Motivation
   to the Team

3 Reasons to Build on Your Strengths

1. Activates the Law of Least Effort

2. Enables Consistently Good Results

3. Gives You the Highest Return

SECURE

State All Your Positions

Examine All Your Actions

Consider All Your Options

Utilize All Your Resources

Remove All Your Nonessentials

Embrace All Your Challenges

About John C. Maxwell

John C. Maxwell is an internationally renowned leadership expert, coach, and author who has sold over 20 million books. Dr. Maxwell founded EQUIP and the John Maxwell Company, organizations that have trained more than 5 million leaders in 153 countries. Every year he speaks to Fortune 100 companies, international government leaders, and organizations such as the United States Military Academy at West Point, the National Football League, and the United Nations. A *New York Times*, *Wall Street Journal*, and *Business Week* best-selling author, Maxwell's T*he 21 Irrefutable Laws of Leadership* has sold more than 2 million copies. *Developing the Leader Within You* and *The 21 Indispensable Qualities of a Leader* have each sold more than 1 million copies. You can read his blog at JohnMaxwellOnLeadership.com, follow him at Twitter.com/JohnCMaxwell, and learn more about him at JohnMaxwell.com.

DON'T LOSE THIS

YOU'RE GOING TO NEED THIS ONE DAY.

Everyone has them… goals, aspirations, dreams. According to John Maxwell, success lies in ten powerful, straightforward questions. *Put Your Dream to the Test* provides a step-by-step action plan that you can start using today to see, own, and reach your dream. More importantly, Maxwell helps you create the right answers, giving you

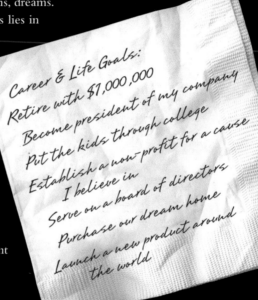

Career & Life Goals:
Retire with $1,000,000
Become president of my company
Put the kids through college
Establish a non-profit for a cause
I believe in
Serve on a board of directors
Purchase our dream home
Launch a new product around
the world

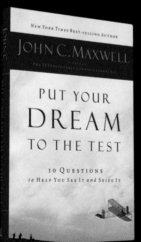

principles and tips to make good decisions and maximize every moment to achieve your dream.

Don't leave your dream to chance. This book is a must-have and can make the difference between failure and success.

Available at www.SUCCESS.com and wherever books are sold.

To discover great way to inspire *friends* and *family,*
or to thank your best *customers* and *employees.*

please visit us at:

www.simpletruths.com

Or call us toll free…

800-900-3427

The
simple truths®
DIFFERENCE

If you have enjoyed this book we invite you to check out our entire collection of gift books, with free inspirational movies, at **www.simpletruths.com.**

You'll discover it's a great way to inspire **_friends_** and **_family,_** or to thank your best **_customers_** and **_employees._**

There is one thing in life that took me a long time to learn, and that's … less is almost always more. This "simple truth" is the foundation on which our company was built. I wanted to create beautiful gift books that anyone can read in less than thirty minutes.

To make each book special, we focused on three things:
1. Great content
2. Great graphics
3. Great packaging to create a **_"wow effect"_**

Satisfied customers are our #1 priority, so I encourage you to give us feedback on how we're doing. If we ever disappoint you, I hope you'll let us know, and we will do everything we can to make it right. Please send your comments to:

Simple Truths Feedback
1952 McDowell Road, Suite 300
Naperville, IL 60563

E-mails us at: **_comments@simpletruths.com_**

or call toll free … **_800-900-3427_**